Thirty-Five Tips for Writing a Brilliant Flash Story

a manual for writing flash fiction and nonfiction

by Kaye Linden

Dedication

Bonnie Ogle http://www.bonnietogle.com

Susie Baxter http://susiehbaxter.com

Marc, Daniel, Russell, and Lewis Linden

The Writers Alliance of Gainesville http://writersalliance.org/

The Bacopa Literary Review
http://writersalliance.org/bacopa-literary-review

About the Author

Kaye Linden has an MFA in short fiction from the Northwest Institute of Literary Arts on Whidbey Island. She is currently studying for a second MFA in writing from Lindenwood University in Missouri because she loves the process of studying and learning. Kaye has taught multiple workshops and classes in flash fiction and nonfiction and has widely published short stories and flash collections. To find out more about Kaye's published works visit her website at www.kayelinden.com.

Table of Contents

4

Introduction

This manual offers the writer a skeletal frame on which to hang a story. A prompt for a writing exercise is offered at the end of each tiny chapter.

Successful flash stories demand knowledge of structure and craft. I have condensed my lecture and workshop notes into specific tips with brief explanations. The information in this manual can apply to creative flash nonfiction or flash fiction stories but for brevity, I will refer to "flash."

Enjoy the art of brevity!

The flash story below, "Agoraclaustrophobia," published in *The Feathered Flounder* (Spring 2012), will demonstrate chapter points.

Agoraclaustrophobia

Kaye Linden

The last time I visited my father, we drove to his childhood home—Thousand Acre Sheep Station, dead center Northern Territory, an endless expanse of red soil and gum trees, fenceless and defenseless from hungry dingoes and buzzards. The open jeep bumped and shook its way through scrubby mulgas, around sinkholes, and over the occasional dead wallaby. I leaned back and studied the blue sky with its wispy white clouds.

"Some people get claustrophobic out here," my father said.

I laughed. "In millions of acres of open land?"

"Yes. It's the lack of familiar things," he said. "There are no cafes or buildings to hold you up in The Great Empty."

"You mean people get agoraphobic," I said.

"Both. Think about it. Anything could happen. The mind expands because there's so much room, so much to fear—caves with ghosts, rock spirits, quicksand. Look how many places there are out here to bury a body. Who would know if you went missing? Who would ever find you? "

I wiped damp palms across my shorts, put on sunglasses, and took a swig from a bottle of beer. Some years ago my cousin had disappeared out here when her tour bus stopped for a water break.

"A sunny day," they'd said. "Just like any other day." She wandered off and never came back from "out there" where it's easy to melt into a chimera, to get lost, lose the trail, meander along the western track instead of the eastern track, sink into the never-never land with its ancient secrets, its unanswered cries from lost children, its whitewashed human bones, its half-decayed cattle with jaws wide open in a scream.

Sun seared into my temples and burned my arms and thighs. Sweat fell in drip, drip, drips, down the front of my T-shirt, like tears for a life cut short. The sun drifted down the horizon. "Put up the windows, Dad."

He laughed. "Hearing voices?"

The engine putt-putt-putted and stalled out.

My father slammed his fist on the dashboard. "I'll be damned. Better brace yourself, Girlie. We have bigger problems than voices." He jumped out of the jeep and opened the hood over the steaming, hissing engine, climbed under the car and around the car, flitting like the shadow of a poltergeist. "The stupid idiot in Alice Springs didn't see a leak," he said. "There's a bloody hole in the radiator hose." My father searched under the seats. "Damn it. No tape. You got any chewing gum?"

I shook my head. "Sorry."

My father pointed to the sky. "Get into the jeep. It's getting dark. I need to find gum tree sap and plug up the hole." He grabbed a flashlight and handed me one. "Back in a jiffy. Sit tight."

Then he was gone. Night bore down like a gigantic stone hand. Hours passed and the flashlight faded. The great emptiness shrouded my body like dirt around a tomb.

"Dad? Where are you?"

Whispers whispered down the hot wind. My fingers grabbed the warm metal of the door handle and I inched out of the car. Bile rose up my throat, sand shifted beneath my feet and images of my father flashed across my vision—my father lost inside a cave with a broken leg, drowned in a sinkhole, kidnapped, shredded by dingoes while searching for his way back to the jeep. Had we missed the signs of sacred land never-never to be crossed at night? Had the spirits cursed us?

When streaks of pink stained the dawn sky, I pulled a heavy blanket around my shoulders, curled into a ball and shivered on the front seat. I imagined my father's jaws wide open in a dying scream.

A shadow fell across the windshield of the jeep, and I sat up, eyes wide open. My father's drawn, white face appeared at my window and I sucked in a gasp of surprise.

"Bloody long night," he said. "It took hours to find a gum tree with sap, and when I did, I was so tired, I fell asleep on the ground. Hope you didn't worry too much," he said.

"No," I said. "Not at all. I fell asleep too." I bit my lip. "Just hungry, that's all."

My father plugged the hole in the radiator hose and we bumped and rocked our way once more towards his childhood home, Thousand Acre Sheep Station, dead center Northern Territory.

Chapter One:

Small Frame

Flash has a small framework, with no more than 1500 words.

Commonly used terms and word counts for the most familiar flash forms include:

1. Drabble: 100 words

2. Dribble: 50 words

3. Flash: 750 to 1500 words

4. Hint: 25 words or fewer

5. Microfiction: 250 words

6. Nanofiction: 55 words

7. Napkin, postcard, six-word, furious, minute fiction: fits on a napkin

8. Prose poetry: variable word counts

9: Sudden fiction: also known as flash fiction and variable up to 1500 words.

Chapter Two:

The House Theory

In Bruce Holland Rogers' *Flaming Arrows,* Kate Wilhelm compares the writing of a very short story to a visit to a house. This theory appears in expanded form in this manual. What follows clarifies the differences between a novel, a short story, and a flash.

Any fiction, no matter what its length, builds on a foundation like a house, and the frame holds up the story. Each detail must offer relevance in the weave of the story. Otherwise you will produce a "Frankenstory." Each piece, each event, each character and action, must fit into the puzzle to produce a whole and perfect building.

The Novel Analogy

You approach a house in the neighborhood.

The family invites you for dinner. The evening offers stories, entertaining characters, conflicts, discussions, and new people. After going upstairs to the bathroom, you sneak a look in the closets and find out how these people live. Are the clothes organized and meticulously hung or are they crammed together in disarray, piles of dirty laundry on the floor?

Short Story Analogy

One evening, you notice the house living-room windows are open and the lights are on. You peer in, able to view only one room; let's say the living room. You hear the conversations and arguments, and witness the character interactions and current events as the characters sit around a coffee table. You recognize a few of the people from dinner the other night and remember one or two of their stories. Your view is limited to the living room.

The Flash Analogy

Tonight, like a voyeur, you peer into the keyhole. The lights are on. Observe the living room happenings through the narrow keyhole frame that limits your view to one tiny fraction of the room.

Now let's apply this third theory and add flesh to its bones, or boards to its frame.

Prompt:

Curl your hand and peer through it as if you are looking through a keyhole. Describe in 15 words or fewer what you see.

Chapter Three:

Slice-of-Life Stories

The slice-of-life story encompasses a small piece of a life: a day, hour, or minute. The writer begins the story in *medias res*, in the middle of things. The writer takes the big picture (the house) stares through the keyhole and focuses on "the middle of things."

In "Agoraclaustrophobia," the scene captures a father and daughter whose car breaks down in the Australian desert. The story represents a slice of life as framed by an imaginary keyhole or a pair of binoculars. I often wish I could be "a fly on the wall." Well, it's the same principle. In a slice-of-life story, you are the fly on the wall, with a narrow view of the events.

Prompt:

Write a flash from the perspective of a fly on the wall in someone's living room. Limit the event to 1 hour in time.

Chapter Four:

Compression

Flash mandates the skill of compression.

That includes writing with compression for the following major story elements:

- plot line of story events or no plot line at all (crosses into prose poetry)

- linked scenes

- story line

- beginning, middle and end

- story arc—a change or epiphany, documented in a small space

- frame

- time and space

- word choice

- word number

- dialogue

- number of characters

What does compression mean? It means constriction or minimalism.

For example:

-the use of a limited number of adjectives and adverbs, or none at all

-a tiny amount of dialogue used only to make a point or move the story forward

-eliminating "the" and "a" when possible

-use of words that carry meaning (word weight)

Minimalism

A cousin to compression, minimalism means tight, sparse writing. It implies the use of only the essential. The essential in flash means using only those elements needed to demonstrate the story. Again, minimalism holds the place of a close cousin to compression. I refer you to the minimalistic writing of Ernest Hemingway in his short story, "Hills Like White Elephants."

Prompt:

Write a story in 25 words or fewer. Cut unnecessary words. Write the story's essence. Now distill it down to 15 words, then 10 words, then 6 words.

Chapter Five:

A Striking Title

The first hook to a story or novel lies in its title.

Consider the following titles:

-"Jabberwocky" by Lewis Carroll

-"An American Blue Comrade's Didactic Evisceration Flaming George's Geopolitical Havens, Hopefully Igniting Jabberwocky Jihad." (from *Sentence: A Journal of Prose Poetics*)

-"The Fish" by Elizabeth Bishop

-"Agoraclaustrophobia" by Kaye Linden

Which title would you pick up and read?

Because the title hooks a reader, it must work hard. Follow up with the promise of a tasty treat. If you want the reader to remember your story, offer a compelling title. "Agoraclaustrophobia" suggests multiple emotional layers. The word hints at abandonment, fear of small and open spaces, imagined terror, and other emotional implications.

Take these steps to choose a title:

-choose a temporary title (a working title)

-once your writing is complete, browse through the piece and choose a few words or a phrase for a permanent title

-Take the main word from your title and search for its synonym in the thesaurus. Can you find a better choice for your title?

-Use a catchy phrase in the story

-Refine the story into its six-word essence and use that as a title

Prompt:

Open the thesaurus or dictionary. Close your eyes. Open at another page or section and circle your finger to a random place on a page and point to a word. Write down the word and repeat this process 3 times.

Mix up the words, use one for a title or to trigger a poem or narrative.

Chapter Six:

The First Few Lines

The first few lines orient the reader to the flash. They present the foundation of the house and give the story line its cornerstone.

In a very short story, begin the action or the first few lines *in media res,* in the middle of things. In "Agoraclaustrophobia," the first two lines set up the story: the where (Australian desert, the last time she visited, driving to his childhood home), when, how, why:

"The last time I visited my father, we drove to his childhood home—Thousand Acre Sheep Station, dead center Northern Territory, an endless expanse of red soil and gum trees, fenceless and defenseless from hungry dingoes and buzzards."

The desolate setting is detailed and the background implied. (The daughter is visiting.) This one introductory sentence offers important information to orient the reader.

Prompt:

Write 3 lines to introduce the reader to the middle of an action scene. Who is in the scene, where does it take place, what happens? Get right into the middle of the action, orient and hook the reader.

Chapter Seven:

I Want It, But I Can't Have It, So I'll...

The very definition of story is "Human desire thwarted."

For a story to offer interest to the reader, conflict must exist. When the main character does not get what he/she wants or needs, conflict arises and launches the story line.

Prevent a character from getting what he wants and you have a story.

The father wants to get to his childhood home but is prevented from doing so when his car breaks down in the middle of the desert and he must search for material to repair the radiator hose. What happens as a result of the breakdown in the desert? The impact of the situation affects not only the father but the daughter. He must search for a solution to a potentially life-threatening breakdown in a desert and the daughter must cope with fears of abandonment.

Prompt:

Recall something you have wanted. What prevented you from getting it?

List the consequences of not getting what you wanted.

Chapter Eight:

Kaye's Rule of Six C's

Character Craves, Cannot have it, Conflict, Consequences, Change.

The Six C's can occur in another order. The three main aspects of a flash are conflict, consequences (what happened to the main character as a result of the problem?) and change. Change must occur in a story. The character might not crave something but have a problem that triggers conflict, consequences and change in that character or the situation.

The father in "Agoraclaustrophobia" has a problem and must leave his daughter alone in the vast desert. As a result, she experiences fear and anxiety. The conflict lies in the life-threatening situation of a breakdown in the desert, but also exists within the daughter who develops anxiety. The father's safe return is the positive outcome, resulting in a change in her anxiety levels and perhaps a return to trust that the father has not abandoned her. In addition, the father's success allows for a positive change in their predicament.

Prompt:

Take a story you have been working on and mark the Six C's in red. If the C's are difficult to find, the story structure needs reworking.

Chapter Nine:

Compressed Scene and Story Line

The most difficult concept for writers to understand is the use of one story line in flash. In this genre, the story line may be likened to a compressed plot or series of events. I have read and reviewed thousands of very short stories by excellent writers who have difficulty maintaining a story's track and introduced other story lines without realizing it. This gives the read an awkward "all over the place" feel. Consider this fact when analyzing a flash.

A writer should be able to recite the story line in one brief sentence which will serve as the skeleton on which to hang the flesh of the story. If it cannot be summed up in a short sentence, "the flash" will morph into "the rambling." Often, writers who do this switch points of view or tenses during the narrative. This creates a tangled mess.

Here is the story line of "Agoraclaustrophobia" in one sentence:

A car breaks down in the desert and the father must leave his daughter alone while she suffers an attack of agoraclaustrophobia, which resolves when her father returns with a solution to their predicament.

If we peer through the "keyhole" of the door, we can witness this slice-of-life event within one frame.

Prompt:

You are at an amusement park with friends. While riding on a Ferris wheel, the machine stops and you are hanging in mid-air. Write a sentence about what happens next and another sentence about what changes.

Chapter Ten:

Stimulus, Response, and Chronological Order

No matter how insignificant the action, maintain chronological order. If chronological order is skewed or out of sequence, the reader will become disoriented to the story, time and place.

Stimulus results in a response. Remember Pavlov's dog? Whenever the bell rings, the dog salivates because he is in the habit of receiving treats at the ringing of a bell.

Stimulus and response

Pay attention to the sequence of one sentence after another and how one action or event triggers the next, and the same for paragraph sequencing.

Examine the following example from "Agoraclaustrophobia" to see how each sentence leads into the next:

"Some people get claustrophobic out here," my father said.

I laughed. "In millions of acres of open land?"

"Yes. It's the lack of familiar things," he said. "There are no cafés or buildings to hold you up in The Great Empty."

"You mean people get agoraphobic," I said.

"Both. Think about it. Anything could happen..."

Here are some of the "beats" or triggers and responses in the story:

Stimulus: Car breaks down in the desert

Response: Father must search for natural adhesive to repair the radiator hose

Stimulus: He leaves the daughter alone in the car

Response: She develops the anxiety of abandonment in the desert at night, feeling closed in by the openness of the desert, imagining terrible scenarios.

Stimulus: The father returns and repairs the hose. The mechanical problem resolves and the father returns in good health

Response: The daughter feels better and they continue on their way

I devised this rule: "For a story to succeed it must follow karmic law. Every action triggers a reaction."

Prompt:

You have won $5000 at the local Walmart store but have only 20 minutes to shop. Using stimulus and response, write the scene.

Chapter Eleven:

Whose Story is It?

The relationship of the father and daughter serves as a character in this story. There is the question of whether or not the father will return.

This is the daughter's story, but at the same time it speaks volumes about their relationship. The focus is on the daughter and her reaction to the problem. The father's conflict might be whether to leave the girl or take her with him. He leaves her alone, which precipitates anxiety. She lacks the trust that he will return. What are the implications of this? For interest, consider the possible backstory of this lack of trust.

Prompt:

Ask "what if?"

What if you were left alone at night in the desert? Left in the streets of a big city? Left with no money? No food? No water? If the story were a long short

story, we could introduce other plot events like these, but it is a flash, and we keep its story line simple.

To stimulate a story ask "what if?"

What if the father and daughter were caught in a flash flood? What if…?

What other examples of agoraclaustrophobia could you write about?

Chapter Twelve:

Moving the Story Forward

In short and long stories, events and sentences advance the story. Compression lies underneath the tiny narrative of flash, and therefore each element must be compressed. Balance each movement forward (desire, event, conflict, consequence, and so on) with a similar length of sentence and structure.

Character action can advance the story or circumstances can move the story along.

Prompt:

Take a short story you have written or one by a famous author and use a red pencil to underline each action that moves the story forward. Circle in orange the events or actions that keep the story stagnant. What can you cut to tighten this into a flash?

Chapter Thirteen:

The Shape of Flash

Do flash stories have a shape? Yes.

Shape equates to structure which reflects plot or connected events.

After years of writing flash, one develops a knack for knowing and reworking the rules. In the beginning, keep events chronological, but don't be afraid to play with the rules after you are comfortable.

Stories have a "shape" on the page and that narrative pattern or line drawing of its beginning, middle, and end must appear balanced. To understand this concept further, I refer you to Kurt Vonnegut's book *A Man Without a Country* in which he outlines "story shapes." The various shapes of stories apply to flash, but the flash shapes are compressed. The story can start with the climax and go down from there, work backward from end to beginning, and not do anything at all in terms of a climactic event. Very short stories don't always contain a plot, but each new word or sentence must move the story line forward. Stories most often consist of a dense core that circles out into a satisfactory ending and often the ending circles back to the beginning.

(Google the term *ouroboros*.)

"If tension falls to zero anywhere in the story, it will probably fail." -C.S. Lewis

Prompt:

For fun, and to understand the sequence of events, write your story's events backward. Diagram the shape of the story with a line pictograph. After that, write the story in chronological order and diagram the story.

Take a look at narrative poetry, line poetry, prose poetry, acrostic poetry, and examine the shapes on the page. Some poems are shaped on the page on purpose to reflect a theme. Experimental flash can do the same within limits. (Check out the concept of "concrete poetry," and apply it to flash.)

Chapter Fourteen:

Consequences of Desire Thwarted

Story formula = Character craves chocolate, cannot have it, creates conflict, causes consequences, then complications, and then change.

Build the story from the foundation up, like building a house.

In "Agoraclaustrophobia," the father and daughter want to reach his childhood home. A car breakdown interrupts their journey.

Much of the conflict or tension in this story is implied in subtext. A tone of foreshadowing lies beneath the narrative. Conflict involves tension and high stakes.

Your character must go through a meaningful change.

In "Agoraclaustrophobia," the daughter confronts her fears of the open spaces that, oddly, can close one in like small spaces. The story resolves because the father returns with a solution to the breakdown and the car starts again. One way this story could improve is by demonstrating the daughter's realization that her fears were unfounded, or by demonstrating, in one line only, that she has accepted her fears, demonstrating another change in the story line. For example, we could add: "Her body relaxed into the cracked leather of the front passenger seat, and she fell asleep, after resolving to accept the outcome."

Prompt:

Invent a character and put an obstacle in the way. What does your main character desire? What blocks the attainment of this desire? Follow the formula above.

Chapter Fifteen:

Characters: How Many is Too Many?

In flash, compress the number of characters to a maximum of three. In the cited story, there are two main characters, the father and the daughter. In addition, we see the landscape, the relationship between father and daughter, and her imagination. Each of these can behave like a character. Certainly, nature plays a wonderful character in this story because it is unpredictable and dangerous. As long as the focus stays on two or three **main** characters, the story will stay focused and balanced. The use of too many names or other supporting characters becomes confusing to the reader of flash. If the reader has to stop and reread to figure out who is who, there is a problem.

Prompt:

Three men climb Everest together as a team in a competition to reach the top. One falls and hurts his ankle. The second discovers his equipment is faulty.

The third has to decide whether to stay and help or forge ahead and win the competition.

Who is the main character and what does he decide?

Chapter Sixteen:

Setting, Weather, and Crowds as Characters

Nature offers terrific characters. Bad weather such as storms and tornadoes set up atmosphere, story, and foreshadowing by their unpredictable behavior. Unusual characters, such as crowds or mountains, can reflect a character's emotions like a mirror. A tense leader will create a tense crowd, and vice versa. The mountains appear dark and gloomy in a storm and can reflect the main character's mood.

The Australian wilderness plays the part of reflecting the daughter's fears.

Prompts:

Your character lives on a remote research facility in the Antarctic. A blizzard approaches. What happens to the main character during the blizzard?

Let a crowd behave badly. How does this offer conflict and tension? What does the main character do to survive the crowd's behavior? What does the crowd want and how will the crowd achieve its desire? What will block the people from getting what they want?

Chapter Seventeen:

A Sense of Meaning

The reader must care about your main character. If the reader doesn't care what happens to him/her, the story won't matter and the reader will not read on. Create a character of interest or a character in an interesting situation.

What are the stakes for the main character?

The higher the stakes, the higher the tension.

In flash, the compressed size limits dynamic change. Change in the character or the situation will not be huge, but the scene can demonstrate a small episode with a situational or character change. In "Agoraclaustrophobia" the father found a solution to the broken-down car while the daughter experienced overwhelming anxiety. This tension was relieved when the father returned. We have a change in situation and a change in character emotion.

Prompts:

Shady, precious, giant. **Write a scene using these 3 words in any order, creating a character of interest.**

Restrict the scene to 100 words or fewer.

Or:

Open a thesaurus and close your eyes. Randomly pick 3 words to combine into a tiny story.

Chapter Eighteen:

Point of View

Point of view confuses most writers. When analyzing flash work which sounds awkward and rambling, I first examine the point of view and whether it offers consistency or sudden switches from one character's viewpoint to another. A multitude of great books have been written about point of view and I will outline the main points to clarify this difficult topic.

Point of view refers to the choice of character through which the reader observes story events. Your story will change depending on the point of view you choose for the storyteller.

Imagine using a telescope to look through the keyhole of your story, zooming in and out with distance and intimacy, through only one character's eyes. In fiction the narrator in first-person viewpoint is a specific character, but in creative nonfiction the narrator is most likely the writer himself.

In "Agoraclaustrophobia," the point of view is the daughter's, and we enter into this viewpoint immediately: "The last time I visited my father…"

The most common viewpoints are:

-First person: *I* or *We*.

-Second person: *You* is used to allow the reader to relate more intimately to the subject, but it is a difficult view to maintain without the reader getting irritated or tired. In a tiny flash, a micro, it might work. I suggest avoiding second person in flash work unless the reader is skilled in its use.

-Third person: *He, she, it*. Close or distant? This can get complicated.

For stories fewer than 1500 words, *keep it simple*. Choose one viewpoint and stick with it for the entire flash. That consistency creates tight, clear writing.

To stay in a close viewpoint, eliminate "I/he/she thought" and stay tight within the action: "Then he was gone. Night bore down like a gigantic stone hand. Hours passed and the flashlight faded. The great emptiness shrouded my body like dirt around a tomb. "Dad? Where are you?"" *("I thought" could be inserted here, but it isn't necessary, so it was cut.)* Whispers whispered down the hot wind."

For a more in-depth discussion about point of view in all genres, I recommend Alicia Rasley's book *The Power of Point of View*, from Writers Digest Books.

Prompt:

Take a flash story that you or a famous author have written and change its point of view to another character's view. How does that change the story? This is one way to stimulate ideas for stories.

Chapter Nineteen:

Tense Choice

Inconsistent tenses create awkward stories. As with point of view, the tense must remain consistent throughout. If you choose past tense, stay with past tense. There are exceptions, such as offering the reader a truism—"Life is short," but I hope the author will not use truisms unless they are the author's unique creation.

My personal preference is to write in past tense, because the reader tends to read past tense with the most ease. "A shadow fell across the windshield of the jeep and I sat up, eyes wide open."

Writing in present tense might have limitations, but it can offer immediacy and increased tension. "A shadow falls across the windshield of the jeep and I sit up, eyes wide open."

Handle past perfect tense with the respect you might give to fire.

"A shadow had fallen across the windshield of the jeep and I sat up, eyes wide open." Why add the "had"? Use it only when necessary and remember one use of "had" might be acceptable, but after the use of one, there's no call to use it again. My rule: No need to use "had" at all in flash stories. If many "hads" appear in the story, rethink its structure. There might be too much backstory or chunks of extraneous information.

Prompt:

Rewrite one of your stories in a different tense. How does it change your story?

Chapter Twenty:

The Ticking Clock

Simply said, this title refers to the ticking away of time, the ticking bomb, time pressure on a character or characters to resolve the problem before the bomb goes off and everyone dies.

Will the father find a solution to a car that has broken down in the middle of a desert before he and his daughter dehydrate, get eaten by crows, collapse, get caught in a flash flood, in a sandstorm, or a thousand other possibilities?

Flash compresses time and begins *in medias res* but even compressed time offers heightened tension, as in "Agoraclaustrophobia."

Time pressure works well. Use it.

Prompt: Up the ante on a flash you have written or take a short story that isn't working and employ the element of time pressure. How does it change the story?

Chapter Twenty-One:

Chekhov's Gun

Delete everything that has no relevance to the story. If you say in the first chapter that there is a gun hanging on the wall, in the second or third chapter, it absolutely must go off. If it's not going to be fired, it shouldn't be hanging there. So said Anton Chekhov.

In 1889, 24-year-old Ilia Gurliand noted these words from Chekhov's conversation: "If in Act One you have a pistol hanging on the wall, then it must fire in the last act."

To translate this idea into flash application, consider the following:

Whispers whispered down the hot wind. I stared at a pair of old army boots in the back seat. My fingers grabbed the warm metal of the door handle and I thought about the sword in the back seat. Bile rose up my throat.

What if the army boots and the sword were never mentioned again in "Agoraclaustrophobia"? You might then wonder what these items had to do with the story. Unless they serve a function later, unless the woman kills an attacking coyote with the sword or wears the army boots to track down her father, there is no point in mentioning them. In a flash story each image must count, and each word works towards the ultimate goal of the story.

Prompt:

Examine one of your stories for information that does not advance the story. Strike it out with a pencil. Now read the story aloud to hear the connection of imagery and information.

Chapter Twenty-Two:

Don't Underestimate Your Reader

You have invited the reader into your story house, and now you are the host. Don't underestimate his intelligence, his ability to clue into the writer's games. For example, honor your contract by offering a great story avoiding stale, clichéd endings or stories that the reader has read over and over again (such as hackneyed love stories, or what happens in Vegas).

True, there are no new subjects, but there are new angles and perspectives on all subjects.

Make sure the reader is oriented to who, what, where, why, and when. Keep the reader interested, but don't beat him over the head with information that he MUST know. Most readers are intelligent people who "get" what the writer is trying to convey. Beware of inserting chunks of explanation, narrative or excess dialogue and backstory. If readers don't understand the story, it is usually because the writer has not produced a clearly written story. For example, if there is more than one story line, or too many characters, or tense inconsistency, or switches in point of view, the reader will feel confused. Don't assume the reader understands or cares *why* you have written the story the way you have. The author has an unwritten contract to offer the reader a clear and interesting story. Keep it clear. Keep it simple. What do you want the reader to take away from this story? What truth or philosophy about life would you like to convey?

Prompt:

Set a timer to 15 minutes. Write a story about a journey. Orient the reader to time and place, but keep the story simple. Make sure the character undergoes a change during the journey. Review and tighten to 100 words. What is the essence of this story in 10 words or fewer?

Chapter Twenty-Three:

Word Weight

Each new word or sentence must advance the story. Each word must weigh heavily with meaning or imagery. Use concrete details and not vague generalizations. This is not always an easy concept to understand. Let's demonstrate with "Agoraclaustrophobia."

Version 1 of paragraph 1:

The last time I visited my father, we drove to his childhood home—Thousand Acre Sheep Station, dead center Northern Territory, an endless expanse of red soil and gum trees, fenceless and defenseless from hungry dingoes and buzzards. The open jeep bumped and rattled its way through scrubby mulgas, around sinkholes and over the occasional dead wallaby. I leaned back and studied the blue sky with its wispy white clouds.

Consider the following alternative without the use of specific concrete detail.

How does it change the meaning and the visual that the reader gets?

Version 2 of paragraph 1:

The last time I saw my father, we drove to his home in the Northern Territory. It was an expanse of desert with trees scattered about. The car drove through the bush and around holes. I leaned back in my seat and watched the sky go by.

Even a simple change of word from "visited" to "saw" changes the meaning of the sentence. Was this the last time I saw him? Visiting implies a visit from somewhere else, as from the U.S.A. to Australia.

The second example paragraph is sterile, without color. It lacks the words that offer the reader an image or scene in his or her head. Word weight includes the elimination of the verb "to be" wherever possible and the use of a meaningful verb instead.

Prompt:

Take a short story you have written and cut it to 2 paragraphs, then to 1 paragraph and then to 1

sentence. Now you have its essence and can re-expand the essence into a story.

Chapter Twenty-Four:

Concrete Detail/Concrete Imagery

Word weight and concrete detail merge. The use of concrete description means the words used have meaning and therefore word weight. For example:

I wiped damp palms across my shorts, put on sunglasses, and took a swig from a bottle of beer. Some years ago my cousin had disappeared out here when her tour bus stopped for a water break.

Compare that with:

I wiped my palm and took a drink from the bottle. Some years ago my cousin had disappeared out here.

Concrete details include "damp palms," the verb "swig," the shorts and sunglasses, the bottle of beer, the tour bus, and the water break. These offer descriptive words that the readers can "see" in their heads. They are not general descriptions but "painted" words that imply much more than they say.

Concrete imagery refers to the pictures the words paint in the reader's head. Consider the following contrasting examples for illustration:

The sun shone down and burned my body. Sweat poured over my skin as the sun went down.

Sun seared into my temples and burned my arms and thighs. Sweat fell in drip, drip, drips, down the front of my T-shirt, like tears for a life cut short. The sun drifted down the horizon.

Which version offers more imagery for the reader? Weigh each word before it goes onto the paper and, when revising, CUT, CUT, CUT.

Prompt:

What kind of day is it today? Go outside and pick a corner of the yard or street. Make notes about what you see. Now write the scene using words that carry weight and contribute to images in the reader's mind. Revise the description with meaningful words

without lengthy description. Allow the reader to "see" the scene just as you did.

Chapter Twenty-Five:

CUT Adverbs and Adjectives

What do you think of the following rendition? Read it aloud:

My annoyed father angrily slammed his large fist on the hard dashboard. He jumped hurriedly out of the yellow jeep and noisily opened the car hood over the steaming, hissing engine and climbed under the hot car and around the car, flitting around like the dark shadow of some poltergeist.

A little excessive?

Now, before referring to "Agoraclaustrophobia," cut the adjectives and adverbs from the above rendition and read the result aloud.

Tightening a piece of flash writing includes cutting most, if not all, of the following:

-adverbs

-adjectives

-unnecessary words such as "the," "a," "an," "as," "like," and "and"

Alternative word choices exist, but you might need to restructure the sentence, rewrite the narrative, rethink how much information the reader needs to hear, or cut some or all of the backstory.

Prompt:

Take a story you have written and read it aloud. Circle in red the unnecessary words. Circle in orange or blue all adverbs and adjectives. Leave only those words that add to the story. Now tighten by cutting most of these words and read the story out loud. Sound better?

Chapter Twenty-Six:

Dialogue

Even the inclusion of one line of dialogue in a flash can offer support for story line and character strength.

Keep dialogue tags simple:

"he said"

"she said"

Simple dialogue tags are not "heard" by the reader's conscious mind. Dialogue tags such as "he screamed," "she called out aggressively" or "he yelled annoyingly" slow down the read, irritate the reader, and overwhelm the story.

Most people use word contractions when they talk, so use them:

"I'm not feeling well," she said.

Keep dialogue realistic. Listen to how people converse with each other in the real world.

Prompt:

Rewrite a story you have written by examining the handling of dialogue.

Apply the above tips to the rewrite.

Chapter Twenty-Seven:

The Verb "To Be"

Among the excellent free tools available to writers is the "Verb-To-Be" Analyzer.

http://www.aztekera.com/tools/tobeverbs.php

Copy and paste a story of any length into the analyzer and get ready for a surprise. You will not believe how much of the narrative contains verbs to be such as "is," "was," "had," and so on. A successful flash contains no more than 20 percent of such verbs. Many of these verbs add nothing to a story and a writer can replace most of them with a meaningful verb.

The Analyzer tool checked "Agoraclaustrophobia," and the following are the "to be" verbs it found, and the statistical analysis of the story:

Matched 'are': how many places there are out here to bury a body.
Matched 'be': be damned...better brace yourself, Girlie.
Matched 'was': Then he was gone.
Matched 'be': we missed the signs of sacred land never-never

to be crossed at night?

Matched 'was': took hours to find a gum tree with sap, and when I did, I was so tired, I fell asleep on the ground.

5 'to be' verbs found in 64 sentences.

7.8% of your sentences have 'to be' verbs.

That's pretty tight writing. I could have revised it "be damned" to "damn it," but the sentence would lose its drama. Use "to be" verbs only when another verb won't work.

Prompt:

Copy and paste a story you are working on into the above website. Surprised at what you discover? Find substitutes for the "to be" verbs and rewrite.

Chapter Twenty-Eight:

Subtext/Implication/Backstory

Flash consists of the unwritten, the unsaid, reading between lines, a hint or two, a tiny signpost, a suggestion. The reader picks up clues that fill in the emotional tone, gaps, or past events of the story. For example:

The last time I visited my father, we drove to his childhood home—Thousand Acre Sheep Station, dead center Northern Territory, an endless expanse of red soil and gum trees, fenceless and defenseless from hungry dingoes and buzzards. The open jeep bumped and shook its way through scrubby mulgas, around sinkholes and over the occasional dead wallaby. I leaned back and studied the blue sky with its wispy white clouds.

Note the subtext or implications:

The narrator is speaking of the last time she visited her father. The questions arise: Why was she visiting? Where was she living? The relationship is long-distance. Where was her mother? It was his childhood home, but not hers. The home was a huge sheep station (ranch) in the center of Australia's desert. Such are the questions the reader might wonder at. Let the reader fill in these blanks with the implied information, the subtext.

Prompt:

Read "Hills Like White Elephants" by Ernest Hemingway. This short story is rich with subtext. Examine how Hemingway handles backstory and implication. Then write a micro-flash of under 250 words in which the writing implies what has happened without stating what happened.

Chapter Twenty-Nine:

Myths and Tales

Rewrite myths and tales, study them, and learn from their story lines. These are the basic stories of heroes and heroines and offer wonderful ideas for twisting, experimentation, and rewriting.

Study Joseph Campbell's model of "the hero's journey." I have adapted the hero's journey to my writing of flash. There are aspects of this journey that offer a solid foundation for story. A perfect example is *Star Wars*.

Prompt:

Write a fairy story or myth from a different perspective, a different point of view, in another tense, or turn the hero into the bad guy and the bad guy into the hero.

Chapter Thirty:

Surprise the Reader

Interesting surprises and twists are not mandatory in flash but create interest and delight for the reader. Don't trick the reader with a predictable twist but offer a subtle or surprise ending or development.

When the father in "Agoraclaustrophobia" left the daughter alone, the reader might sense surprise because that appears to be odd behavior for a father, but the eccentricities of human behavior offer interest.

Another tool for surprising a reader lies in the language, specifically the reworking of clichés. Clichés are hackneyed, tired sayings that have lost their impact over time. Avoid them. Use fresh expressions to offer an image: "half-decayed cattle with jaws wide open in a scream."

This image extends to later in the story when the daughter imagines her "father's jaws wide open in a dying scream."

Part of the surprise in the story is the combination of the concepts of claustrophobia and agoraphobia. The surprise lies in the fact that people can and do feel claustrophobic in open spaces. Some people feel that way out in the middle of the ocean where "there's so much room, so much to fear…"

Prompt:

Take an old story and cross out clichés with a red pen. What can you change to offer a fresh phrase, surprise, or perspective? Try changing the point of view, or change the main character into one of the minor characters. How would another character's perception change the story? Surprise yourself.

Chapter Thirty-One:

Sentence Structure and Phrases

Flash has its own rhythm, produced by compressed sentences and phrases that give a particular rhythm and pacing to the sound of very short prose. Depending on the writer's intention, breaking grammar rules, such as eliminating commas or periods, and the use of repetition can offer a wonderful sense of urgency in a compressed narrative flash.

Prompt:

To practice writing from a different angle, write a series of questions mixed or not mixed with a couple of sentences. Place a tiny twist at the end.

For example:

"What am I doing here? Where is he? What time is it? Why is he so late? Should I leave? Why are my palms sweating? Am I going to throw up? Did he

dump me? Do I have the wrong restaurant or the wrong time? Why is that waiter looking at me? It's because I'm on my fourth whiskey, isn't it? Do I have on too much lipstick? Maybe my lipstick's a mess. I'd better take a look in the mirror. What the heck happened to him? Where the...Oh, there he is now.

Hi there. How are you? Sit down. What did you say? I look tense? I don't know why. I was just relaxing with a drink."

You get the picture: Up the ante by playing with sentence structure and rules. Great stories arise from playing with structure.

Here is an example of a flash fiction I wrote published in 2015 in *The Rat's Ass Review*. Note the pacing, the breaking of grammatical rules, and the minimal dialogue. This flash piece also works as a prose poem.

The Wet

Kaye Linden

Ma, aboriginal toothless shaman, throws her ninety-nine-year-old bones into the front seat of the windowless jeep and jams her foot down on the accelerator. Desert driving, flash flood driving with rising waters at the hubcaps and trackless tires sinking fast into whirling mud swirls. Sky blows blacker than her skin, wind whips red welts into her hanging jawline, Ma pains on, the falling down mulga-wood homestead in sight, too distant on the boiling roiling horizon, straight one line straight line straight ahead no wavering but straight the shortest distance between two points. Rain pouring pouring pouring torrential blinding into her old eyes she keeps driving driving driving through driving rain to get home home home before the rusty untrusty jeep sinks deeper into sudden ravines and eddies that grow rounder and hungrier taking but seconds to fill holes in the ground. She reaches the leaning splitting woodpile homestead in the raining pouring driving wet, the wet, the Alice Springs wet, the wet that only those people who live in The Alice know, understand, and brace for each five years. The homestead swirls under water, turning and topsy and turvy and upside down and inside out, her broken armchair floating in pieces, rusted pots afloat, the sheltie dog swimming to meet her, tongue lolly-gagging hello, eyes yellowed and alight, but Ma's jeep coughs and rattles and chokes and sinks with Ma not a swimmer but a hiker with strong old hiking legs, army boots that anchor her down into water. She grabs the old dog's matted wet back and they both go down and around, thunder announcing their pending demise, kookaburra laughter long gone, gasping and hacking and face just up level with water, eyes turned up to the heavens, to the ancient gods whose hands don't reach out. "Where are you, you bastards?" Ma shouts to the sky and the dog whines a carping whittling fingernails-down-the blackboard kind of cry that only those from The Alice understand, only those who have seen white brittle bones bleached in desert heat and sun after those on a run for their lives have lost. Panting dog and woman cling to each other, going down, going down, going down but with a whoosh and a gurgle the water stops, the rain stops, the rivers cease running, the widening knife-like gaps in red mud close and Ma stands on her feet again, holding the dog in her arms, sinking to ankles in army boots, but standing in remnants of a flash flood in Australian desert,

here now,

there now,

gone.

Chapter Thirty-Two:

Fixed and Experimental Forms

As you have seen in the above chapter, flash lends itself wonderfully to experimentation. The writer can try any playful writing in a short piece because there is not a lot of time or emotional energy invested. If it doesn't work, it's easy to rewrite.

Here's an interesting fixed form for you to work with:

With each new sentence, double the word count of the sentence before.

An example:

One. One story. Of black teeth revealed. Black teeth revealed behind luscious wet red lips. Lips parted, seductive, her chiseled face in a bar, mirrored behind one glass smudged with lipstick.

Fixed forms are fun. They unleash the wild muse. For more on fixed forms, check out the works cited page.

Here's an example of one of my experimental flash nonfiction pieces that won first prize in *The Bacopa Literary Review*'s 2015 annual contest for creative nonfiction. I wrote the flash in one sentence, an experimental handling of form. The one sentence structure reflects the continuity of the tattoo patterns over a man's body.

The Linear and Circular One Sentence of Tattoo Designs over His Body

Kaye Linden

David runs through Goliath with a sword but Goliath stands strong, his sandal strap broken by the tip of steel, blood at the ankle, a few hairy hairs shaved from his knee, but he stays upright, an angel of the bottomless pit, the hero of one tattooed story with its swirly blue ink marks connecting letters over each vertebra of spine, letters that spell out "Never again" and "violence is not the way" with the word "way" spiraling down the spinal column, each lumbar protrusion covered with inky lines and letters, until the ink bleeds into Popeye opening a can of worms on the left buttock, and Olive smoking a pipe on the right buttock, the pipe smoke weaving a curly-Q whirly loop and merging into Spider man's web on the left thigh, the web webbing its lacey stars and stripes network down and around the shins, around and around until it splatters inky blue spiders over the gastrocnemius of the left calf muscle and covers the ankles and feet with tiny Buddhas that continue under the feet and protect the soles of feet and the soul of the man, (but how on earth did he suffer through that painful tattooing?) and seen from under jeans, the feet appear dirty and garden-weary but when rolled up, like Eliot's Prufrock on the beach, the design works magic like a waterfall works magic, a watershed of rainbow colors spreading in a rainfall of tattoo etchings across his massive shoulders, his sharp abs, pecs, scapulae, triceps, biceps, quadriceps, embellishing and fertilizing all six hundred and thirty-nine muscles, a landscape of linked vessels and lines emerging whenever he takes off his shirt, a rare occurrence, only when the gorgeous and the giants come to town and he dreads the time when he runs out of tattoo space on his skin and he must share his stories with his words instead.

Prompt:

Turn the timer on for 5 minutes. Write about an epiphany or "aha" moment you have had, but write it in a long sentence. Don't think too much. Just write.

Chapter Thirty-Three:

Mastering the Genre

Read, read, read flash fiction and nonfiction flash stories and learn from the masters.

Borrow techniques, initiate variations and deviate with your ideas while you practice from famous examples and develop a unique flash style. Join flash critique groups either in your town, online or take classes. Start your own critique group.

At the end of this manual, I have included a list of resources that include a sprinkling of flash writers and their work.

Prompt:

Study a tiny story by a famous flash writer and substitute each word with your own. Warning: Be careful not to plagiarize or copy any other writings.

There are sites online, such as Grammarly.com, where you can copy and paste your work to make sure you have not plagiarized by mistake.

Chapter Thirty-Four:

The Four Keys to Revision

C.O.A.P.

Cut: eliminate unnecessary words, backstory, fillers

Organize: ideas into a consistent and cohesive story line

Add: fill gaps in clarity, add a word or line of dialogue to clarify a confusing story

Polish: perfect the grammar, check for consistency in point of view and tense, and the story's clarity. Review the tips in this manual and apply to your story. Voila.

Time to submit the story for publication!

Chapter Thirty-Five:

A Few Tips About Prose Poetry

Length does not define prose poetry, but length is one parameter that defines flash stories.

Poetry is about language and poetic device such as similes, alliteration, sentence structure, broken lines, verses, imagery.

Language in flash is concise and intense as in poetry, but does not flow into poetic devices or employ traditional forms, such as villanelles or sonnets. However, one can experiment with fixed forms in flash.

Flash most often carries a story line involving conflict and a change in the main character or situation. Poetry need not.

Poetry emphasizes the placement of words and is defined by line breaks.

Narrative poetry, prose poetry, and flash stories can overlap.

In poetry, the description can be a technique in and of itself and offers an overall image for the reader. In flash, the description must advance the narrative.

Poetry need not and often does not contain a plot. Flash usually, but not always, contains a compressed plot.

When a reader picks up poetry, he/she has a different set of expectations than on reading flash stories. He/she expects a story when reading flash, but does not expect a story when reading poetry.

Prose poetry usually features full sentences with no forced line breaks or a mixture of the two. Prose poetry offers an overall "feel" or image, as with poetry.

Prose poetry asks readers to lay aside their rules and judgment and prepare for a surprise, a wild ride. Readers must make larger jumps than with flash, and read more deeply into subtext.

Prose poetry lends itself well to experimental writing and mixed forms.

Above all, remember to read your work aloud because this is the best way to hear mistakes, catch skips in rhythm or misplaced beats, hear inconsistent pacing, tense or point of view shifts.

Please feel free to visit me at www.kayelinden.com and email questions or comments to kaye@kayelinden.com. I invite you to sign up for my blog on my website.

Works Cited:

Aztekera.com: http://www.aztekera.com/tools/tobeverbs.php

Hemingway, Ernest. *The Complete Short Stories of Ernest Hemingway*. New York: Scribner's, 1987. Print.

Hemingway, Ernest. *Men without Women*. New York: C. Scribner's Sons, 1927. Print.

Linden, Kaye. "Agoraclaustrophobia." *Feathered Flounder*. n.p., 2013. Web.

Linden, Kaye. "The Linear and Circular One Sentence of Tattoo Designs over His Body." *The Bacopa Literary Review* 2015 (2015): Print.

Linden, Kaye. "The Wet." *Rat's Ass Review*, 2015. Web.

Millier, Brett Candlish. *Elizabeth Bishop: Life and the Memory of It*. Berkeley: University of California, 1993. Print.

Vonnegut, Kurt, and Daniel Simon. *A Man without a Country*. New York: Seven Stories, 2005. Print.

Rasley, Alicia. *The Power of Point of View: Make Your Story Come to Life*. Cincinnati: Writers Digest, 2008. Print.

Rayfield, Donald. *Anton Chekov, a Life*. New York: Henry Holt, 1997. Print.

Simmons, Ernest J. *Chekhov: A Biography*. Chicago: University of Chicago, 1962. Print.

Campbell, Joseph, Phil Cousineau, and Stuart L. Brown. *The Hero's Journey: The World of Joseph Campbell: Joseph Campbell on His Life and Work*. San Francisco: Harper and Row, 1990. Print.

Rogers, Bruce Holland. *Flaming Arrows*. Eugene, OR: IFD Pub., 2001. Print.

"Grimm's Fairy Tales." *List of Fairy Tales*. n.p., n.d. Web. 15 Oct. 2015. http://www.grimmstories.com/en/grimm_fairy-tales/list.

Rogers, Bruce Holland. "One Loopy Sentence at a Time." *One Loopy Sentence at a Time*. Flash Fiction Online, Sept. 2008. Web. 16 Oct. 2015.

Sentence: A Journal of Prose Poetics #5, 2007.

Vonnegut, Kurt, and Daniel Simon. *A Man without a Country*. New York: Seven Stories, 2005. Print.

I wish to thank editor Catherine Rankovic, who worked so diligently with me on the edits and formatting. Visit her at BookEval.com.

CPSIA information can be obtained
at www.ICGtesting.com
Printed in the USA
LVHW022241140721
692685LV00011B/805